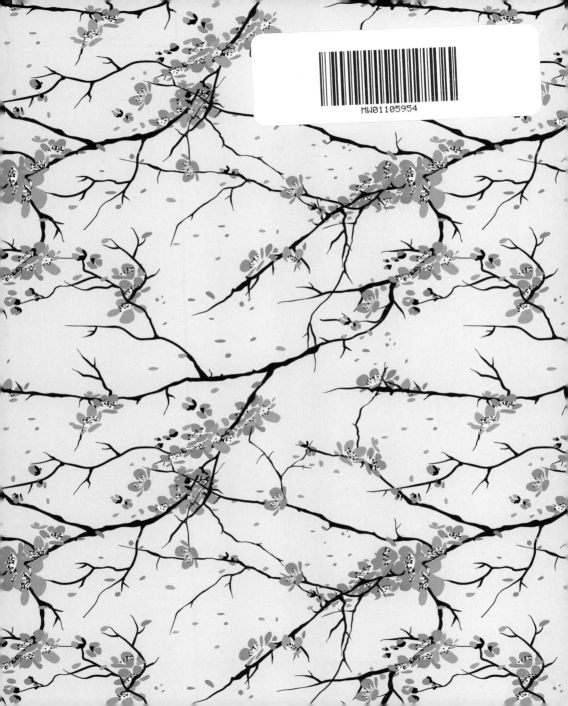

101

ORIGAMI
Decorations

Published by Hinkler Books Pty Ltd
45–55 Fairchild Street
Heatherton Victoria 3202 Australia
www.hinkler.com.au

hinkler

Written by Katie Hewat
Types of folds, symbols and folding-instructions by Matthew Gardiner and Katie Hewat
Images © Hinkler Books Pty Ltd or Shutterstock.com
Photography © Hinkler Books Pty Ltd 2008, 2014, 2016
Internal design: Fiona Finn

What is Origami?

rigami is a curious sounding word because it is not English, but Japanese in origin. Ori, from the root verb oru, means 'to fold' and kami is one of the many terms for paper. In the purest renditions, origami creates an intended shape from a single sheet of paper with no cutting, gluing, taping or any other fastening device allowed.

The origin of origami

No-one really knows when origami was invented. We do know that paper had to be invented first, so we can safely say that it is less than 2000 years old, but an exact date, even to the nearest century, cannot be authentically established.

One reason for origami's hazy history is that for many centuries there was almost no documentation on how to do it. The oldest book known to contain origami-like instructions, the *Kanamodo*, is from the 17th century, yet older woodblock prints also show paper folding. The oldest origami book written for amusement is the *Hiden Senbazuru Orikata*, from 1797. The title roughly translated means, 'the secret technique of folding one thousand cranes'. There are around one hundred designs known as 'traditional origami', which were passed from hand to hand in Japanese culture: typically a mother showing a child, or children sharing this knowledge among themselves.

After the Second World War people from around the world started to visit Japan in greater numbers, and Japanese citizens increased their travel to other countries. Oragami began to spread around the world, especially through the hands of exchange students. These young ambassadors of Japanese culture could communicate through origami – a finished model could be given as a gift, cementing a friendship through paper folding.

Origami Folds

Book fold

Valley fold one edge to another, like closing a book.

Cupboard fold

Fold both edges to the middle crease, like closing two cupboard doors.

Blintz

Fold all corners to the middle. This was named after a style of pastry called a blintz.

Inside reverse fold

The spine of the existing fold is reversed and pushed inside.

Pleat fold

Valley fold, then mountain fold to create a pleat.

Petal fold   The petal fold is found in the crane and lily base.

1

2

3

4

5

Fold top layer to the centre crease.

Fold and unfold the top triangle down. Unfold flaps.

Lift the top layer upwards.

Step 3 in progress, the model is 3-D. Fold the top layer inwards on existing creases.

Completed petal fold.

Squash   A squash fold is the symmetrical flattening of a point. The flattening movement is known as squashing the point.

1

2

3

5

Pre-crease on the line for the squash fold.

Open up the paper by inserting your finger. Fold the paper across.

As you put the paper in place, gently squash the point into a symmetrical shape.

Completed squash fold.

Origami Symbols

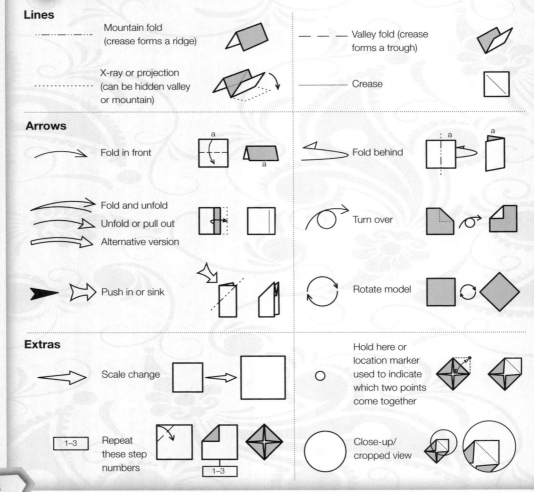

Lines

Mountain fold (crease forms a ridge)

Valley fold (crease forms a trough)

X-ray or projection (can be hidden valley or mountain)

Crease

Arrows

Fold in front

Fold behind

Fold and unfold

Unfold or pull out

Alternative version

Turn over

Push in or sink

Rotate model

Extras

Scale change

Hold here or location marker used to indicate which two points come together

Repeat these step numbers

1–3

Close-up/ cropped view

Paper Heart

The heart is one of the simplest pieces you'll need in your origami tool kit. Hearts can be used in a whole range of ways, from forming card decorations and bunting to carrying secret messages of love! Unlike all of the other models in this book, the heart uses rectangular paper. Try A4 (letter) or A5 (half-letter) sized paper.

1

Book fold and unfold. Turn over.

2

Fold in half lengthways and unfold.

3

 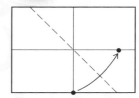

Valley fold a diagonal so that the vertical crease touches the horizontal crease.

4

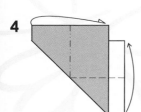

Fold the corners together, noting the mountain fold on the upper part and the valley fold on the lower part.

5

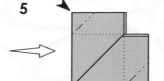

Inside reverse fold the points. The edge of the crease should match with the inner layer of the paper.

6

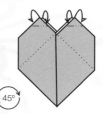

Fold the tips inside the heart.

Hearts in a Jar

Create this little knick-knack to use as the centrepiece for a table or just as a whimsical design feature for your room. The instructions in this book use two different types of coloured paper, but you can choose to have just one type or a variety of colours and patterns.

You will need

- Origami paper, A5 size, 12 sheets (6 sheets each of two colours)
- Wooden kitchen skewers, 12
- Adhesive tape
- A small jar, bottle or vase
- A piece of lace or ribbon that is longer than the circumference of the jar to be able to tie in a bow

1 Make 12 paper hearts using the origami paper.

2 Carefully fasten the hearts to the pointy ends of the wooden skewers using adhesive tape.

3 Wrap the ribbon or lace around the jar and tie the ends into a bow.

4 Place the heart-topped skewers in the jar and arrange so that the fronts of all of the hearts face outwards.

Simple Star

There are many variations on the classic origami star, so we have picked a nice and easy one to get you started. These stars can be used to decorate just about anything.

1

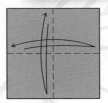

Begin coloured side up.
Book fold and unfold. Turn over.

2

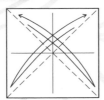

Fold and unfold diagonals.

3

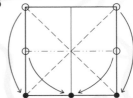

Collapse on existing creases.

4

Fold and unfold both edges into the middle to make creases.

5

Pleat fold into the centre on both sides.

6

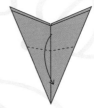

Fold the top section down along the dotted line as shown.

7

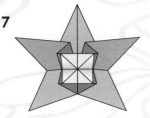

Press out to form the five points of the star. The centre should form a square shape as shown.

8

Turn over to reveal your finished star.

Star Wreath

This simple star-wreath is perfect for hanging on your bedroom door. Choose festive colours for the holiday season or any of your favourite colours or patterns for a fun and fabulous year-round piece.

You will need

- Origami paper, 150 x 150 mm (6 x 6 in), 12 sheets
- Craft glue
- A hole punch
- String or ribbon, approx. 40 cm (15.75 in) in length
- Removable adhesive wall hooks, 1 (optional)

Handy Hint

These stars are great for other types of decorations too. Try a single star threaded with ribbon as a hanging ornament, or a star in place of a bow on your gifts.

1. Make 12 simple stars using the origami paper.

2. Take one star and tuck the left-hand point under the right-hand top flap of a second star.

3. Position at a slight angle, so that the first star sits a little lower than the second star, rather than in a straight line.

4. Put a small dab of glue between the two stars where they overlap and hold together for around 30 seconds until the glue dries.

5. Repeat the process with the remaining stars, forming a circle, until the last star meets up with the first star.

6. Use the hole punch to make a hole through the top of the wreath. Choose a spot where two stars overlap, as this will help it hold together better than a single layer. You could also put a little tape over this area (front and back) and then punch the hole through, so it's stronger.

7. Thread your string or ribbon through the hole and tie the ends together. Your wreath is now ready to hang on a door hook or nail!

Party Dress

Paper dresses are oh-so-sweet and super easy to make! They're great to use for general decoration or can be used to dress paper dolls.

1

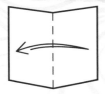

Start blank side up.
Book fold and unfold.

2

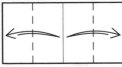

Cupboard fold and unfold.

3

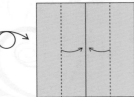

Turn paper over so that coloured side is facing up. Fold the outer creases in to meet the centre crease.

4

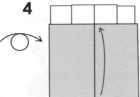

Turn over again so that blank side is facing up. Bring the bottom edge almost up to the top, but leave a 1 cm (0.5 in) gap at the top. Crease firmly along the bottom.

5

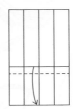

Bring the top layer back on itself and make a crease leaving about 1 cm (0.5 in) at the bottom.

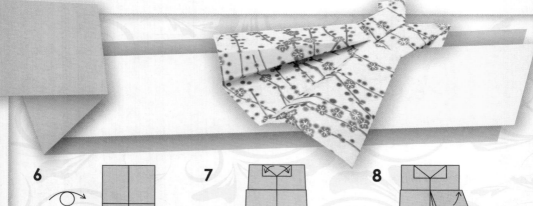

6

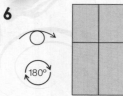

Turn over again and rotate so that the bottom is now at the top. Your dress should now have two sections, the bodice and the skirt, separated by a waist line just above the centre.

7

Make a collar by folding down the two top centre corners.

8

Take the top right-hand corner of the skirt part of the dress and pull it up and out slightly to create an angle and give the skirt shape.

9

Repeat step 8 on the left side.

10

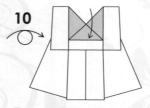

Turn over. Gently pull down the centre of the top and fold down the two triangles on the sides to create a V-neck.

11

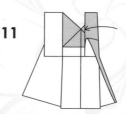

Fold the right side of the bodice across to the middle, up to the point where the coloured section meets the blank section. Make a straight crease down to the waist line.

12

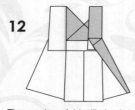

The previous fold will also bring the skirt in at the waist to form an angle. Fold along this angle to complete the right side of the skirt.

13

11–12

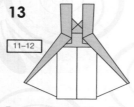

Repeat steps 11–12 on the left side.

14

Turn over. Fold the white sections at the very top back onto themselves to create cap sleeves.

Party Dress Bunting

This mini clothes line features five super-sassy party dresses. Hang it in a line above your bed or desk to create a cool crafty vibe in the room. You should be able to get the twine and mini pegs at your local arts and craft store.

You will need

- Origami paper, 150 x 150 mm (6 x 6 in), 5 sheets (5 different patterns)
- Paper twine, approx. 2 m (6.5 ft) in length
- Mini craft pegs, 10
- Removable adhesive wall hooks, 2 (optional)

1. Fold five party dresses using the origami paper.

2. Leaving 50 cm (20 in) of twine at both ends, use the wooden pegs to fasten the dresses to the twine, spacing each dress around 25 cm (10 in) apart.

3. If using the removable wall hooks, fasten them wherever you would like to hang your bunting. The two hooks should be around 1.5 m (5 ft) apart.

4. Tie the two ends of the bunting to the hooks.

Lily

This pretty flower is deceptively simple and looks effective by itself or in a big bunch.

1

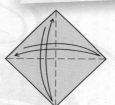

Begin coloured side up. Fold and unfold diagonals. Turn over.

2

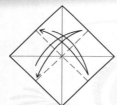

Book fold and unfold.

3

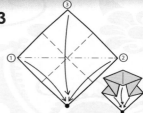

Bring three corners down to meet bottom corner. Start with corners 1 and 2 together followed by corner 3.

4

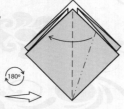

Rotate 180°. Pre-crease then squash fold.

5

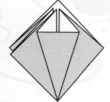

Repeat step 4 on the other three sides.

6

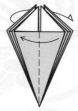

Turn top and back layer over.

7

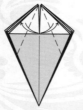

Fold top layer edges to meet the middle.

8

Fold and unfold the top layer only to the centre crease.

9

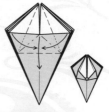

Petal fold; pull down the top layer, and fold the sides to the middle. Lastly, make the mountain folds.

10

Completed petal fold.
Fold the triangle flap upwards.

11

8–10

Repeat steps 8–10 on the
three remaining sides.

12

Fold one layer in front
and behind.

13

Fold edges to the middle,
thinning the lily. Repeat on
the other three sides.

14

Make a soft, curved valley
fold on all four sides to
open out the lily.

Framed Flower Art

This pretty-as-a-picture wall art makes a great feature for any room of the house. Unlike natural flowers, these blooms won't fade!

You will need

- Origami paper, 150 x 150 mm (6 x 6 in), 3 sheets in bright, pretty colours
- Scissors
- Green paper, 1 sheet
- Green pipe cleaners, 3
- Double-sided adhesive tape
- A small or medium picture frame in any style you like
- A piece of patterned paper to fit inside the photo frame
- Craft glue

Safety Hint

Be careful when handling and disposing of the glass. Children should ask for an adult's assistance.

1 Make three lilies using the origami paper.

2 Using the scissors, carefully cut out six leaf shapes from the green sheet of paper.

3 Cut the very tip off the end of each lily.

4 Wrap a piece of double-sided tape around the end of each pipe cleaner and insert one into each of the holes you created in the ends of the lilies. Secure firmly.

5 Remove the backing and the glass from the photo frame. Discard the glass.

6 Place your patterned paper on the frame backing, then replace the backing in the photo frame.

7 Use the craft glue to stick your three flowers into the frame, ensuring that you glue the stem parts only. The bottoms of the pipe cleaners should touch the bottom of the inside of the frame.

8 Glue one paper leaf onto each side of the three stems.

9 Slightly bend the pipe cleaners at the top so that the flowers point out of the frame.

Butterfly

The butterfly is a simple yet striking origami figure. Just like real butterflies, origami butterflies look best with bright colours and patterns.

1

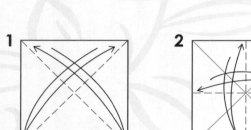

Fold and unfold diagonals.

2

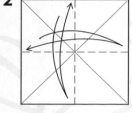

Book fold then unfold.

3

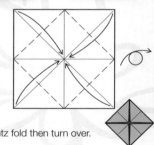

Blintz fold then turn over.

4

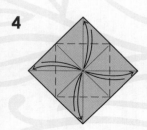

Blintz fold then turn over.

5

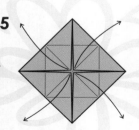

Completely unfold out to a flat sheet.

6

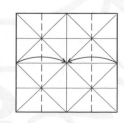

Fold sides to the middle.

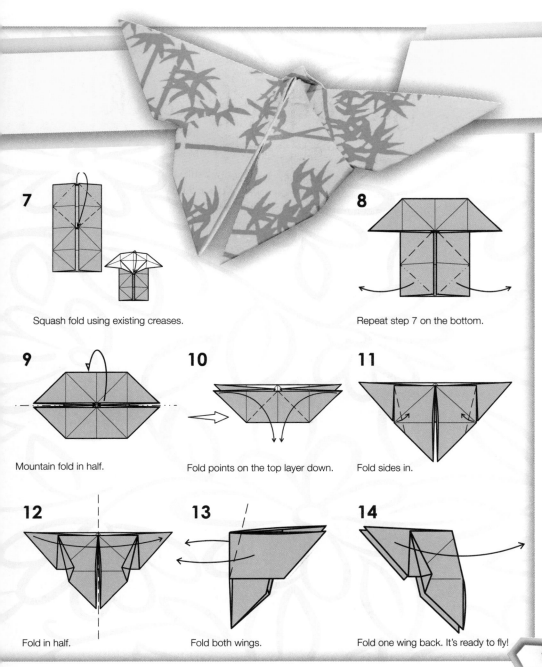

7

Squash fold using existing creases.

8

Repeat step 7 on the bottom.

9

Mountain fold in half.

10

Fold points on the top layer down.

11

Fold sides in.

12

Fold in half.

13

Fold both wings.

14

Fold one wing back. It's ready to fly!

Butterfly Branch

This decoration features an explosion of butterflies on a natural tree branch. Hang it on a wall or place it in a vase to create a centrepiece with total wow-factor.

You will need

- Origami paper, 75 x 75 mm (3 x 3 in), 19 sheets in a variety of bright colours
- A small, dead, fallen tree branch with lots of individual twigs
- Wood glue

1 Make 19 butterflies using the origami paper.

2 Clean up your tree branch, dusting off any dirt or bugs.

3 Trim the branch if necessary so that it forms a nice overall shape. Remove any excess twigs to thin it out if the branch is too full.

4 Glue your butterflies onto your tree branch, spacing them randomly to provide depth and interest.

5 Place your branch in a striking vase or jug, or attach it to a wall.

Handy Hint

If you are hanging your butterfly branch on a wall, try tying some paper twine in a bow around the stem for added effect.

Masu Box

This is the original origami box, which is super practical and very easy to make. These boxes are great for storing just about anything, or you could even make lids and use them as gift boxes. To make a lid, simply take a piece of paper slightly larger than the one you are using for your box, and make a second box which will fit snugly over the first one when turned upside-down.

1

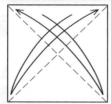

Begin blank side up.
Fold and unfold diagonals.

2

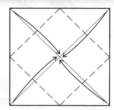

Blintz fold.

3

 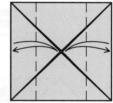

Cupboard fold and unfold.

4

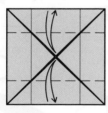

Cupboard fold and unfold
the other edges.

5

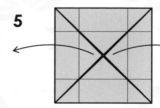

Unfold two side points.

6

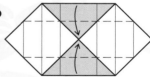

Fold on existing creases.

7

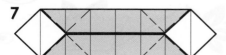 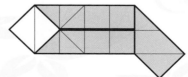

Fold and unfold on diagonals.

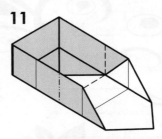

8

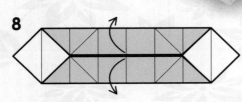

Lift sides to 90°.

9

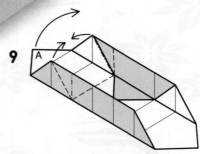

To make the side of the box, lift point A upwards – the existing sides will naturally collapse to points.

10

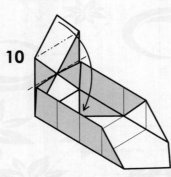

Fold the point down into the box, and press the point to the centre.

11

Repeat steps 9–10 on the remaining side.

Storage Shelves

These sensational little storage shelves are a must-have for any bedroom. Use them to store jewellery, craft supplies, paper clips, beauty items or anything at all!

You will need

- Paper, 250 x 250 mm (10 x 10 in), 6 sheets
- A shoe box or other cardboard box, big enough to fit six masu boxes
- Thick card, enough to create two shelves inside your shoe box.
- Strong adhesive tape
- Craft glue
- Paper for decorating the outside of the shoe box
- Lace or ribbon, approx. 25 cm (10 in) in length

1. Make 6 masu boxes using the origami paper.

2. Cut two pieces of card to the same size, just a little longer than the length of your shoe box. These will form the shelves for your masu boxes.

3. Fold down both edges of the shelves so that the shelves fit snugly into your box, with a flap hanging down on each side.

4 Use adhesive tape or glue to stick the shelf flaps to the sides of your box. Make sure the two shelves are spaced evenly.

5 Cover the shoe box with your patterned paper, sticking it down with craft glue.

6 Cut short pieces of lace or ribbon, approx. 4 cm (1.5 in) long, to use as handles.

7 Stick the handles onto the front of your masu boxes using craft glue.

8 Insert your boxes into your shelves and fill with all of your favourite things!

Handy Hint

Shoe boxes, and other cardboard boxes, come in many different sizes. Measure your outer box first, as you may need to use larger or smaller paper to make your masu boxes the right size for your shelves.

Paper Crane

A symbol of hope and peace, the paper crane is the ultimate origami model. An ancient Japanese legend says that anyone who folds 1000 cranes may be granted a wish.

1

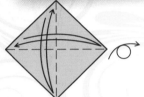

Start coloured side up.
Fold and unfold diagonals.
Turn over.

2

Book fold and unfold.

3

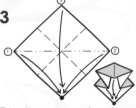

Bring three corners down to meet bottom corner. Start with corners 1 and 2 together followed by corner 3.

4

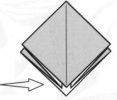

Completed preliminary base.

5

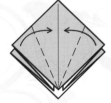

Fold top layer to the centre crease.

6

Fold and unfold the top triangle down. Unfold flaps.

7

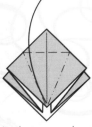

Lift the top layer upwards.

Step 7 in progress, the model is 3-D. Fold the top layer inwards on existing creases.

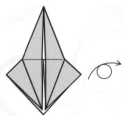

Step 7 completed, the model will be flat. Turn over.

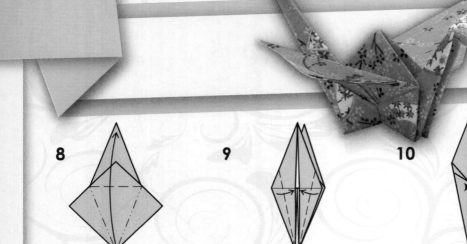

8

Repeat steps 5–7 on this side.

9

Narrow the bottom points on the top layer only. Repeat behind.

10

Reverse fold the bottom point upwards.

11

Your model should look like this. Repeat on the other side.

Completed body.
The next steps focus on the head and wings.

12

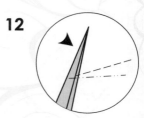

Reverse fold the point to create the head.

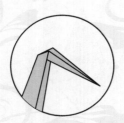

Head completed.

13

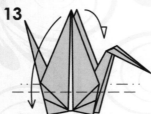

Fold wings down.

14

Pull the wings gently to shape the body.

3-D Crane Mobile

Once you've perfected folding the paper crane, you can create this amazing 3-D artwork. Hang it in the corner of your bedroom to create an eye-catching feature piece.

You will need

- Origami paper, 150 x 150 mm (6 x 6 in), 24 sheets in total (3 colours x 8 sheets each)
- Origami paper, 75 x 75 mm (3 x 3 in), 12 sheets in total (1 colour x 6 sheets; 1 colour x 4 sheets; 1 colour x 2 sheets)
- Scissors
- Paper twine, approx. 3 m (10 ft) in length
- Wooden dowel, 40 cm (15.75 in) long, 3
- Spool of fishing line
- Large sewing needle
- Removable ceiling hook

1 Use the origami paper to fold 36 paper cranes.

2 Cut the twine into three equal lengths. Place the three pieces of wooden dowel together to form a triangle. Use the ends of the three pieces of twine to bind the three corners of the triangle together.

3 Laying the triangle flat, pull up the remaining lengths of the three pieces of twine so that they meet about 50 cm (20 in) above the centre of the triangle. Tie the three pieces together at this point. There should be more length left above this knot – this is what you'll use to secure your artwork to the ceiling when it is complete.

4 Cut a length of fishing line around 1 m (3.25 ft) long and carefully thread it through the sewing needle.

5 Push the sewing needle through one of the larger cranes, so that it goes in at the top point of the crane's back and comes out the small opening at the bottom. Pull the fishing line through until only the last 30 cm (1 ft) remains.

6 Tie a triple knot in the fishing line just below the crane.

7 Thread the needle through three more cranes of the same colour, leaving a 20 cm (8 in) gap between and tying a triple knot below each one.

8   Repeat steps 4–7 until you have created six separate strings of four cranes each.

9   Then repeat steps 4–7, but this time using the smaller cranes. You should end up with two strings of three cranes in one colour, two strings of two cranes in the second colour, and one string of two cranes in the final colour.

10   Tie the strings of cranes onto the wooden triangle as per the following diagram.

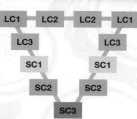

LC1 = Large size, colour 1
LC2 = Large size, colour 2
LC3 = Large size, colour 3
SC1 = Small size, colour 1
SC2 = Small size, colour 2
SC3 = Small size, colour 3

11   Fix a removable hook to part of the ceiling. Children should get an adult to do this. Use the ends of the twine to tie the art to the hook, ensuring that the front of the triangle is facing towards the centre of the room.

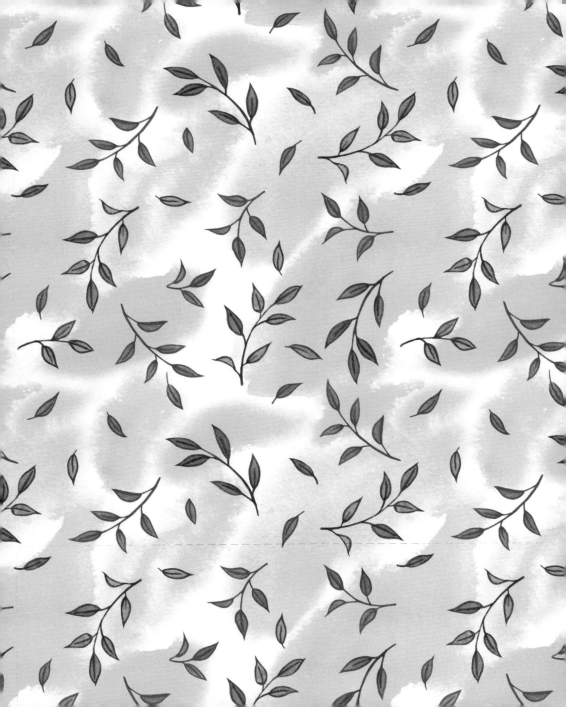

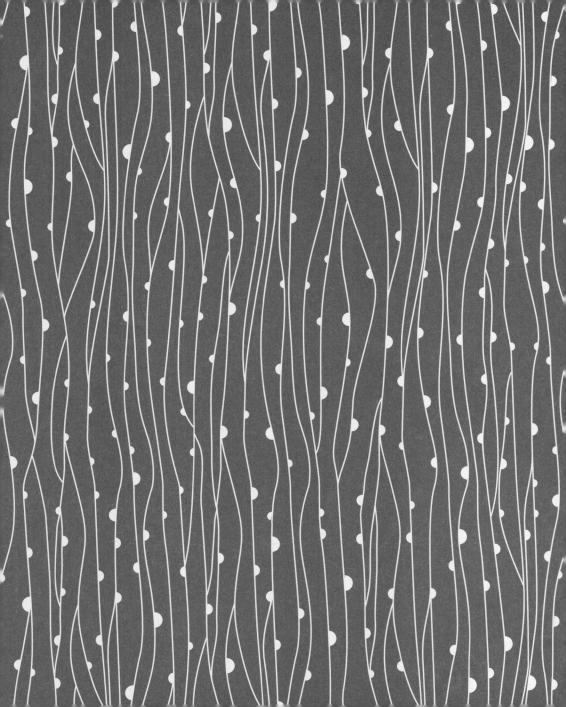

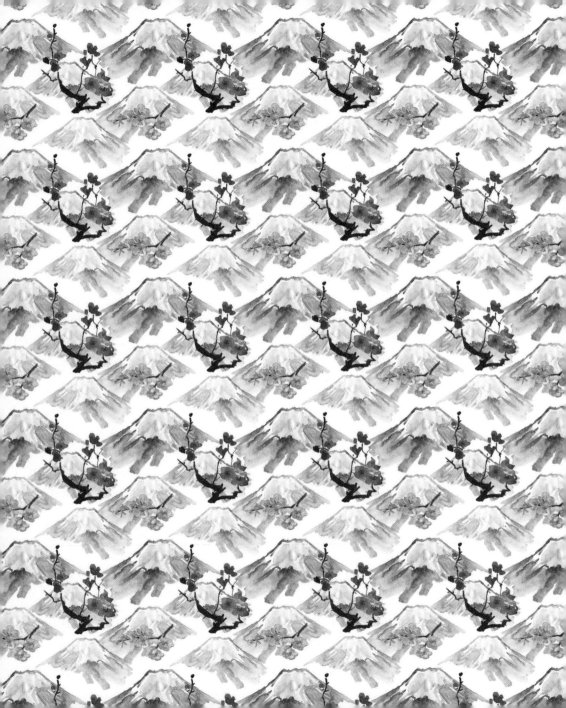

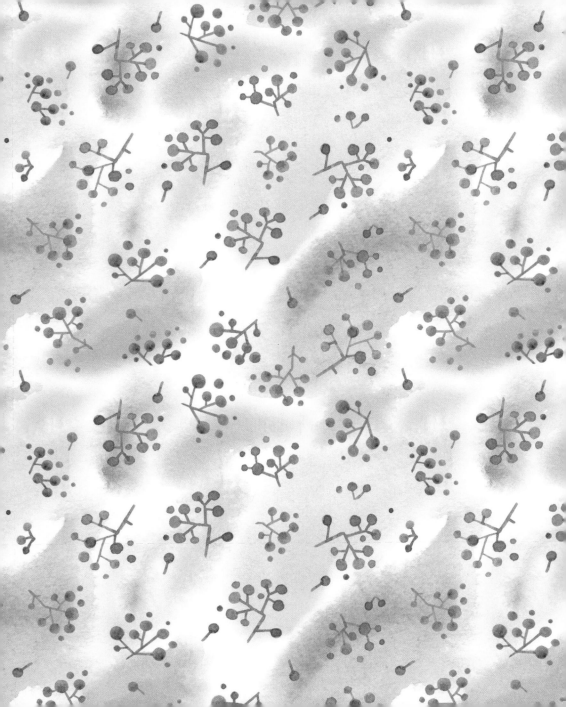

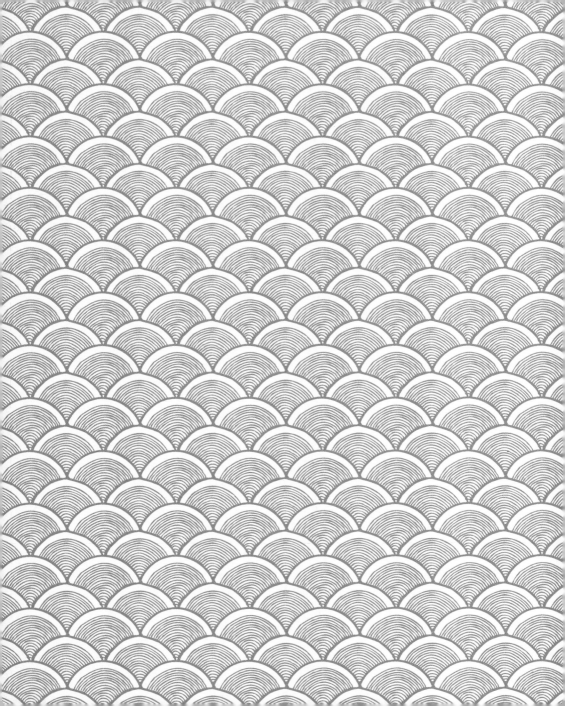

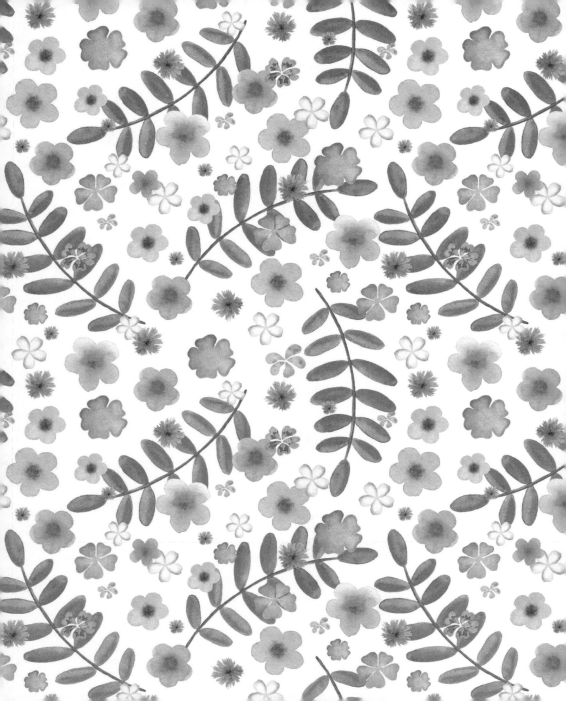

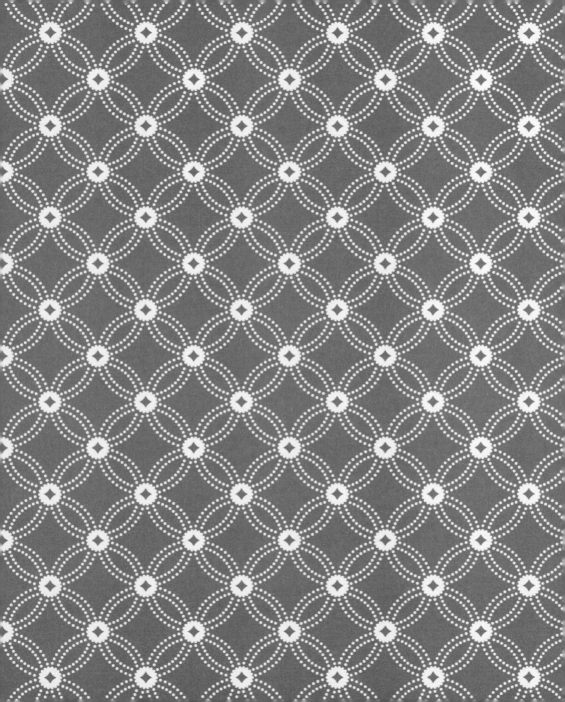

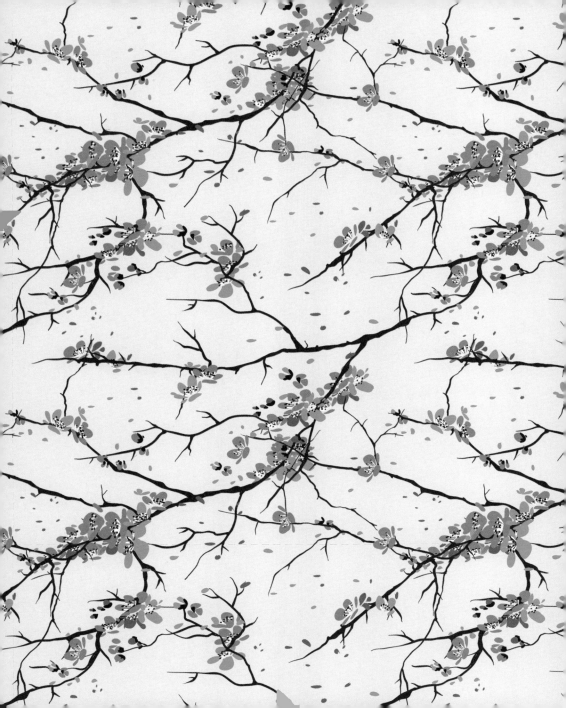

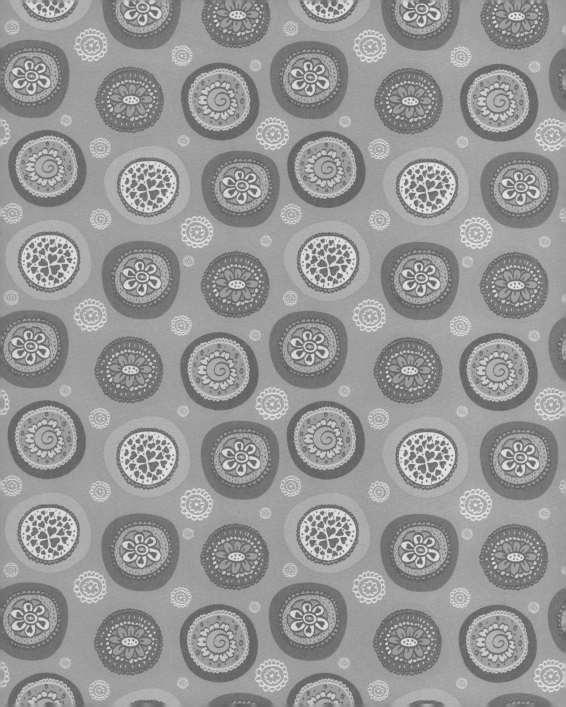

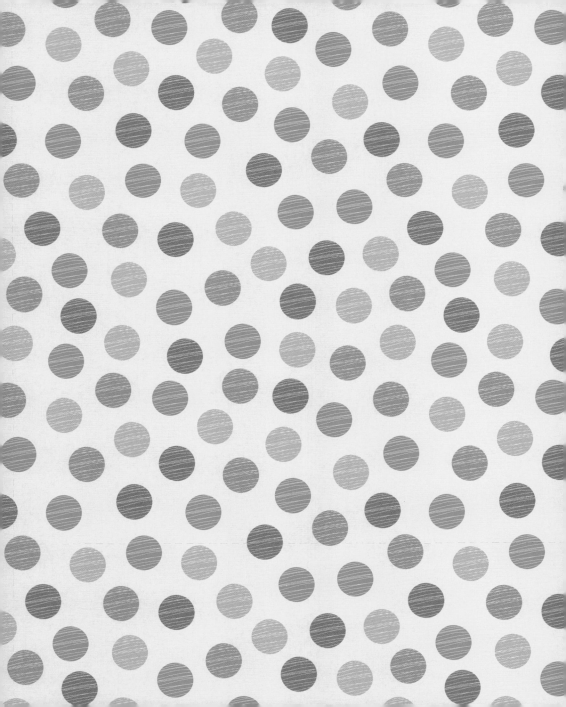

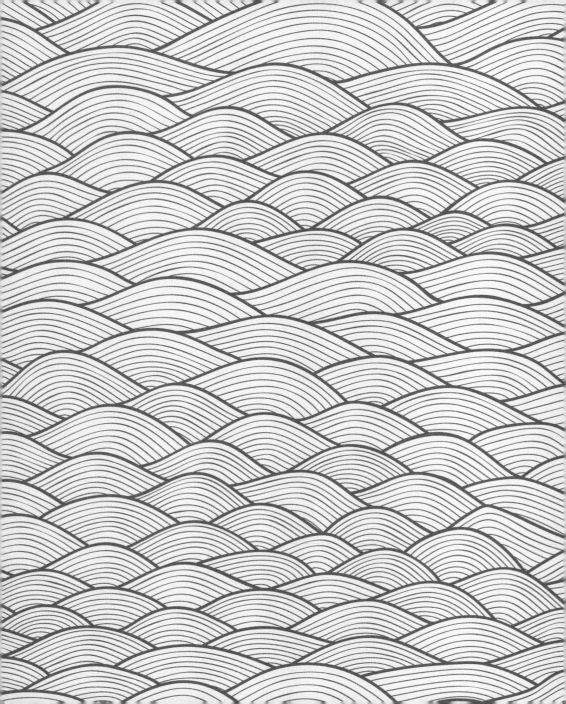

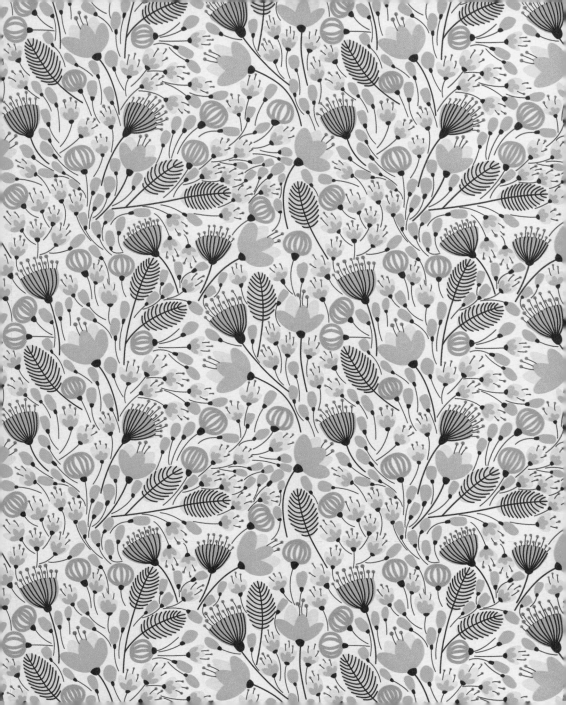

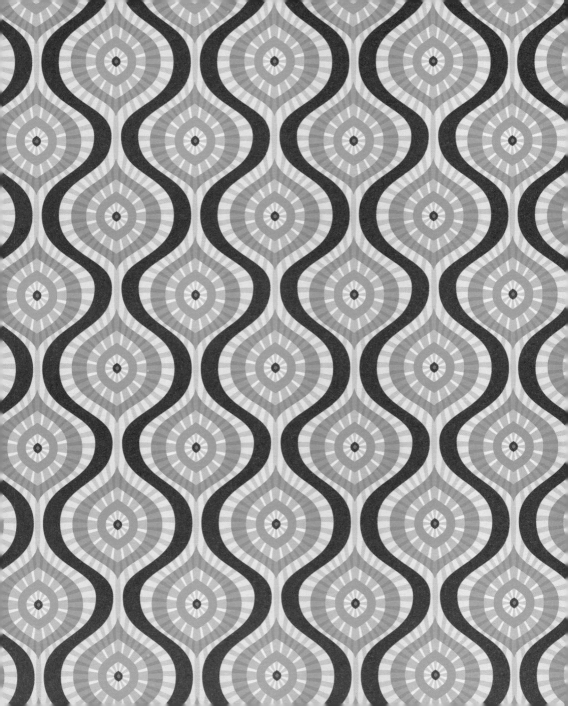

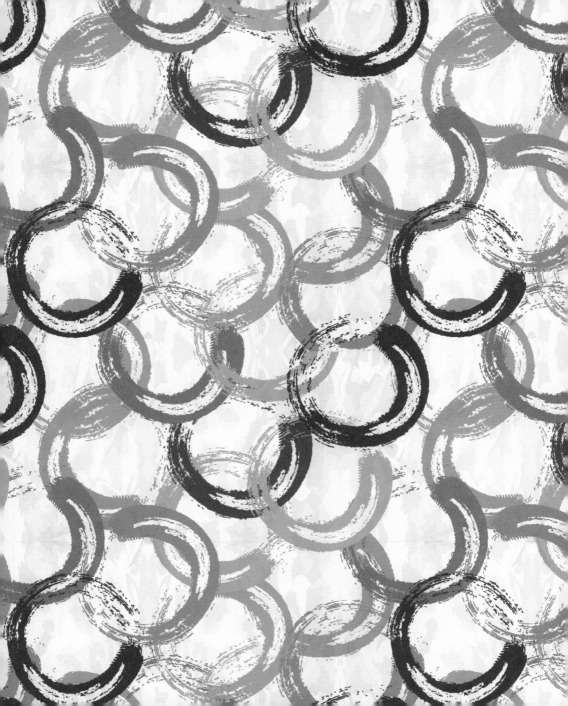

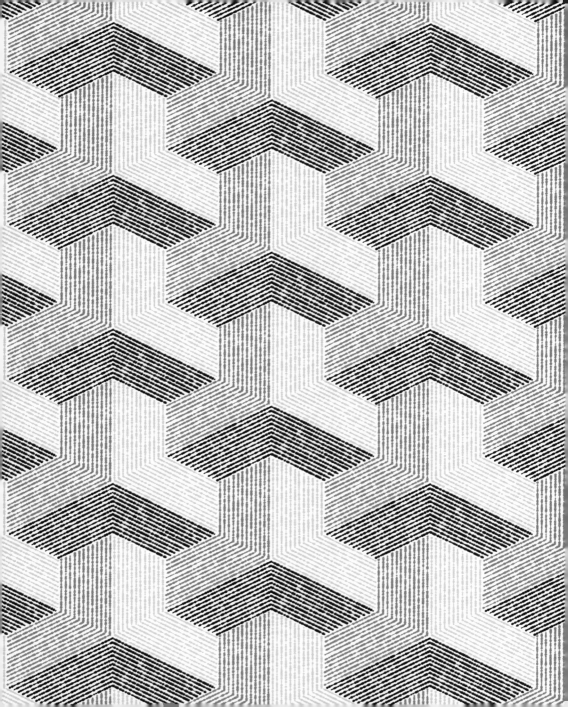

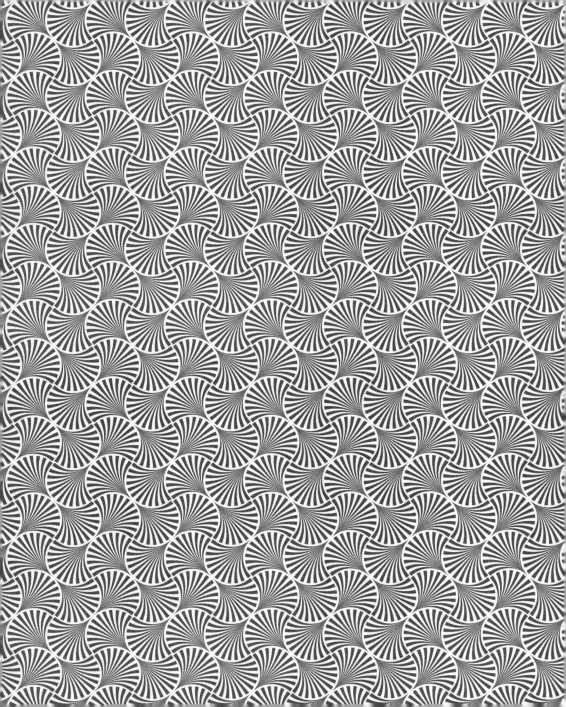

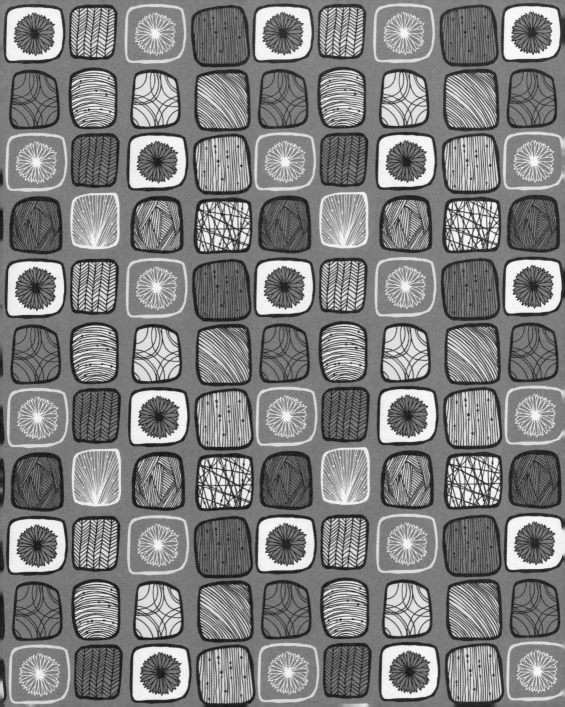

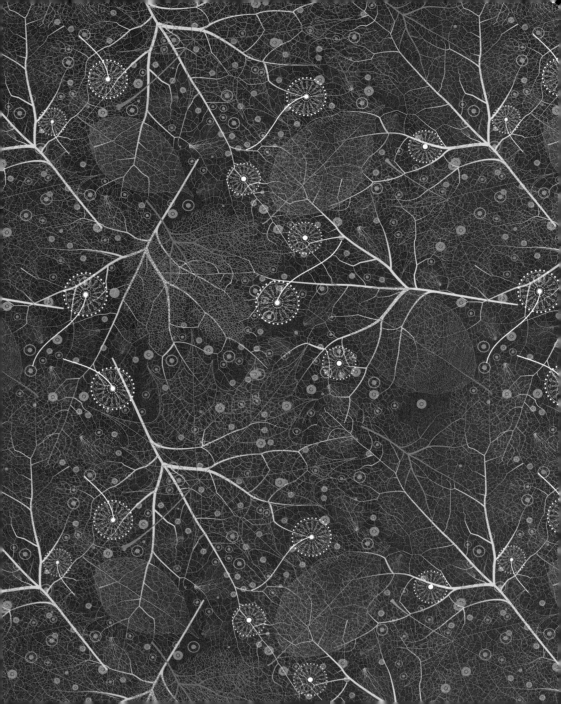

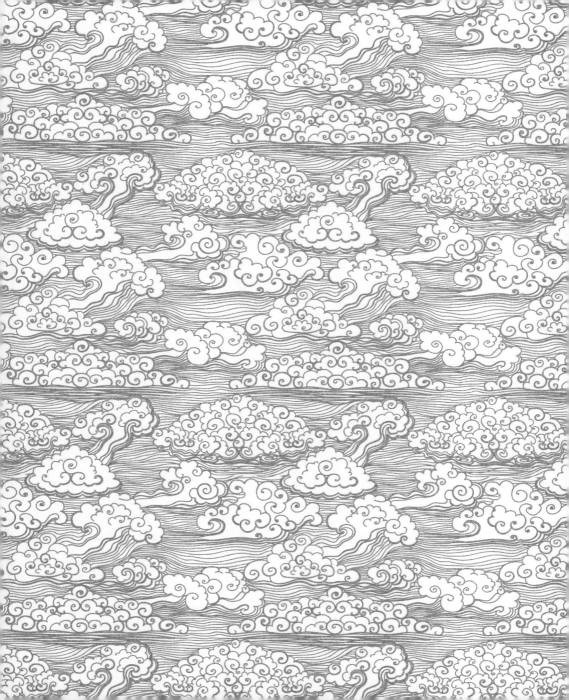